# Ghost Train Alexander

# RYAN WATTERSON

SET IN THE VIBRANT AND CULTURALLY RICH COUNTRY OF MODERN-DAY MEXICO, "THE GHOST TRAIN OF MEXICO: A MURDER MYSTERY" BEGINS WITH ALEXANDER THE GREAT, A RENOWNED HISTORIAN AND ARCHAEOLOGIST, RECEIVING AN INVITATION TO GIVE A LECTURE ON ANCIENT CIVILIZATIONS AT A PRESTIGIOUS CONFERENCE IN MEXICO CITY. INTRIGUED BY THE OPPORTUNITY TO EXPLORE A NEW CULTURE AND LEARN MORE ABOUT THE HISTORY OF THE REGION, ALEXANDER ACCEPTS THE INVITATION AND MAKES HIS WAY TO MEXICO.

UPON ARRIVING IN MEXICO CITY, ALEXANDER IS GREETED BY THE WARM HOSPITALITY OF THE LOCALS AND THE VIBRANT ENERGY OF THE CITY. AS HE PREPARES FOR HIS LECTURE, HE IMMERSES HIMSELF IN THE RICH HISTORY AND CULTURE OF MEXICO, VISITING MUSEUMS, EXPLORING ANCIENT RUINS, AND MEETING WITH LOCAL ARCHAEOLOGISTS.

ONE DAY, WHILE VISITING A MUSEUM DEDICATED TO THE ANCIENT CIVILIZATIONS OF MEXICO, ALEXANDER COMES ACROSS AN OLD MAP THAT DEPICTS THE ROUTE OF A LEGENDARY GHOST TRAIN THAT IS SAID TO ROAM THE MEXICAN COUNTRYSIDE. INTRIGUED BY THE LEGEND, ALEXANDER DECIDES TO TAKE A TRAIN RIDE THROUGH MEXICO, HOPING TO EXPERIENCE THE COUNTRY'S HISTORY AND CULTURE FIRSTHAND.

AS HE BOARDS THE TRAIN, ALEXANDER IS FILLED WITH EXCITEMENT AND ANTICIPATION FOR THE JOURNEY AHEAD. LITTLE DOES HE KNOW THAT THIS TRAIN RIDE WILL NOT ONLY BE AN ADVENTURE THROUGH THE BEAUTIFUL LANDSCAPES OF MEXICO BUT ALSO A THRILLING MURDER MYSTERY THAT WILL TEST HIS DETECTIVE SKILLS AND BRAVERY.

ALEXANDER BOARDS THE TRAIN, A VINTAGE LOCOMOTIVE THAT EXUDES AN AIR OF NOSTALGIA AND MYSTERY. THE TRAIN IS FILLED WITH AN ECLECTIC MIX OF PASSENGERS, EACH WITH THEIR OWN STORIES AND REASONS FOR TRAVELING THROUGH MEXICO. AMONG THEM ARE A GROUP OF ARCHAEOLOGISTS, LED BY DR. ELENA RAMIREZ, A RENOWNED EXPERT IN MESOAMERICAN CIVILIZATIONS. THERE IS ALSO A MYSTERIOUS WOMAN, DRESSED IN BLACK AND WEARING A VEIL, WHO SITS ALONE IN THE CORNER OF THE TRAIN CAR, HER EYES HIDDEN BEHIND DARK SUNGLASSES. AND THEN THERE IS THE WEALTHY BUSINESSMAN, MR. RODRIGO SANCHEZ, WHO IS TRAVELING WITH HIS ENTOURAGE OF BODYGUARDS AND ASSISTANTS.

As the train departs from Mexico City, Alexander settles into his seat and strikes up a conversation with Dr. Ramirez and her team. They discuss their shared passion for archaeology and the ancient civilizations of Mexico, and Alexander is impressed by their knowledge and expertise. He learns that they are on their way to explore a newly discovered archaeological site in the remote mountains of Central Mexico.

AS THE TRAIN TRAVELS THROUGH THE MEXICAN COUNTRYSIDE, ALEXANDER IS CAPTIVATED BY THE STUNNING LANDSCAPES AND THE RICH HISTORY THAT SURROUNDS HIM. HE GAZES OUT THE WINDOW AT THE ANCIENT RUINS THAT DOT THE LANDSCAPE, IMAGINING THE LIVES OF THE PEOPLE WHO ONCE INHABITED THESE ANCIENT CITIES AND TEMPLES.

AS NIGHT FALLS, THE TRAIN MAKES A STOP AT A REMOTE STATION IN THE MOUNTAINS. THE PASSENGERS DISEMBARK TO STRETCH THEIR LEGS AND ENJOY THE COOL MOUNTAIN AIR. ALEXANDER TAKES THE OPPORTUNITY TO EXPLORE THE STATION, WHICH IS SURROUNDED BY DENSE FOREST AND TOWERING CLIFFS. HE IS STRUCK BY THE EERIE BEAUTY OF THE PLACE AND THE SENSE OF HISTORY THAT SEEMS TO HANG IN THE AIR.

SUDDENLY, A PIERCING SCREAM BREAKS THE SILENCE, AND ALEXANDER RUSHES BACK TO THE TRAIN. HE FINDS A COMMOTION IN THE TRAIN CAR, WHERE MR. SANCHEZ HAS BEEN FOUND DEAD, HIS BODY LYING IN A POOL OF BLOOD. THE PASSENGERS ARE IN SHOCK, AND DR. RAMIREZ AND HER TEAM ARE ALREADY EXAMINING THE BODY, TRYING TO DETERMINE THE CAUSE OF DEATH.

AS ALEXANDER LOOKS AROUND THE TRAIN CAR, HE NOTICES SOMETHING STRANGE.
THE MYSTERIOUS WOMAN IN BLACK IS NOWHERE TO BE SEEN, AND HER SEAT IS
EMPTY. COULD SHE HAVE SOMETHING TO DO WITH MR. SANCHEZ'S DEATH? AND
WHAT ABOUT THE OTHER PASSENGERS? COULD ONE OF THEM BE THE KILLER?

ALEXANDER KNOWS THAT HE MUST ACT QUICKLY TO SOLVE THE MYSTERY BEFORE THE TRAIN REACHES ITS FINAL DESTINATION. WITH THE HELP OF DR. RAMIREZ AND HER TEAM, HE BEGINS TO PIECE TOGETHER THE CLUES AND UNRAVEL THE SECRETS THAT LIE HIDDEN IN THE SHADOWS OF THE MEXICAN MOUNTAINS.

AS THE PASSENGERS AND CREW GATHER AROUND MR. SANCHEZ'S LIFELESS BODY, ALEXANDER TAKES CHARGE OF THE SITUATION. HE INSTRUCTS THE TRAIN CONDUCTOR TO SECURE THE TRAIN AND NOT TO LET ANYONE OFF UNTIL THE AUTHORITIES ARRIVE. DR. RAMIREZ AND HER TEAM CONTINUE TO EXAMINE THE BODY, WHILE ALEXANDER INTERVIEWS THE OTHER PASSENGERS AND THE TRAIN CREW.

THE CREW MEMBERS ARE QUESTIONED FIRST, BUT THEY ALL HAVE ALIBIS AND NO APPARENT MOTIVE FOR THE MURDER. NEXT, ALEXANDER TURNS HIS ATTENTION TO THE OTHER PASSENGERS. HE QUESTIONS THE ARCHAEOLOGISTS, WHO WERE IN THE DINING CAR AT THE TIME OF THE MURDER, AND THEY CONFIRM EACH OTHER'S ALIBIS. THE MYSTERIOUS WOMAN IN BLACK IS NOWHERE TO BE FOUND, AND NO ONE REMEMBERS SEEING HER LEAVE THE TRAIN.

AS ALEXANDER CONTINUES TO INVESTIGATE, HE DISCOVERS THAT MR. SANCHEZ HAD BEEN INVOLVED IN ILLEGAL ANTIQUITIES TRAFFICKING AND HAD MADE ENEMIES IN THE ARCHAEOLOGICAL COMMUNITY. COULD ONE OF THE ARCHAEOLOGISTS BE THE KILLER, SEEKING REVENGE FOR MR. SANCHEZ'S EXPLOITATION OF ANCIENT ARTIFACTS

AS THE TRAIN TRAVELS THROUGH THE NIGHT, ALEXANDER IS HAUNTED BY THE IMAGE OF MR. SANCHEZ'S LIFELESS BODY AND THE MYSTERY OF HIS DEATH. HE KNOWS THAT HE MUST SOLVE THE CASE BEFORE THE TRAIN REACHES ITS FINAL DESTINATION, OR THE KILLER COULD ESCAPE JUSTICE.

AS DAWN BREAKS, ALEXANDER GATHERS THE PASSENGERS AND CREW IN THE DINING CAR AND REVEALS HIS FINDINGS. HE ACCUSES ONE OF THE ARCHAEOLOGISTS, DR. CARLOS HERNANDEZ, OF BEING THE KILLER. DR. HERNANDEZ DENIES THE ACCUSATION, BUT ALEXANDER PRESENTS THE EVIDENCE: A BLOODY KNIFE FOUND IN DR. HERNANDEZ'S POSSESSION AND THE DISCOVERY THAT DR. HERNANDEZ HAD BEEN IN CONTACT WITH MR. SANCHEZ BEFORE THE MURDER.

DR. HERNANDEZ BREAKS DOWN AND CONFESSES TO THE MURDER. HE REVEALS THAT HE HAD DISCOVERED MR. SANCHEZ'S ILLEGAL ACTIVITIES AND HAD CONFRONTED HIM ABOUT IT. WHEN MR. SANCHEZ THREATENED TO EXPOSE HIM, DR. HERNANDEZ LASHED OUT IN A FIT OF RAGE AND KILLED HIM.

AS THE TRAIN PULLS INTO ITS FINAL DESTINATION, ALEXANDER REFLECTS ON THE EVENTS OF THE PAST NIGHT. HE IS GRATEFUL FOR THE OPPORTUNITY TO HAVE SOLVED THE MYSTERY AND BROUGHT THE KILLER TO JUSTICE. AND AS HE STEPS OFF THE TRAIN, HE KNOWS THAT HE WILL NEVER FORGET THE GHOSTLY RIDE THROUGH THE MEXICAN MOUNTAINS AND THE MURDER THAT UNFOLDED ON THE TRACKS.

ALEXANDER BEGINS HIS INVESTIGATION BY EXAMINING THE CRIME SCENE. HE CAREFULLY OBSERVES THE POSITION OF THE BODY, THE BLOOD SPATTER PATTERNS, AND ANY POTENTIAL CLUES LEFT BEHIND. HE ALSO TAKES NOTE OF THE OTHER PASSENGERS' REACTIONS AND MOVEMENTS DURING AND AFTER THE MURDER.

AS HE INTERVIEWS THE PASSENGERS AND CREW, ALEXANDER NOTICES THAT SOME OF THEM SEEM NERVOUS OR EVASIVE. HE ASKS THEM ABOUT THEIR WHEREABOUTS AT THE TIME OF THE MURDER AND IF THEY SAW OR HEARD ANYTHING SUSPICIOUS. HE ALSO ASKS IF ANYONE HAD A MOTIVE TO HARM MR. SANCHEZ.

DR. RAMIREZ AND HER TEAM ASSIST ALEXANDER IN EXAMINING THE BODY. THEY FIND THAT MR. SANCHEZ WAS STABBED MULTIPLE TIMES WITH A SHARP OBJECT, LIKELY A KNIFE. THEY ALSO DISCOVER THAT THE WOUNDS WERE INFLICTED FROM BEHIND, INDICATING THAT THE KILLER MAY HAVE APPROACHED MR. SANCHEZ FROM BEHIND AND SURPRISED HIM.

AS ALEXANDER CONTINUES TO GATHER EVIDENCE AND QUESTION THE PASSENGERS, HE DISCOVERS A FEW KEY PIECES OF INFORMATION. HE LEARNS THAT MR. SANCHEZ HAD BEEN INVOLVED IN ILLEGAL ANTIQUITIES TRAFFICKING AND HAD MADE ENEMIES IN THE ARCHAEOLOGICAL COMMUNITY. HE ALSO LEARNS THAT THE MYSTERIOUS WOMAN IN BLACK HAD A SECRET CONNECTION TO MR. SANCHEZ, WHICH SHE HAD TRIED TO KEEP HIDDEN.

As Alexander pieces together the clues, he begins to suspect that the murder may have been premeditated. He wonders if the killer had been planning to kill Mr. Sanchez for some time and had chosen the train ride as the perfect opportunity to carry out the crime.

As the train travels through the night, Alexander is determined to solve the case before the train reaches its final destination. He knows that time is running out, and the killer could escape justice if he doesn't act quickly.

With the help of Dr. Ramirez and her team, Alexander gathers the passengers and crew in the dining car and reveals his findings. He accuses one of the archaeologists, Dr. Carlos Hernandez, of being the killer. Dr. Hernandez denies the accusation, but Alexander presents the evidence: a bloody knife found in Dr. Hernandez's possession and the discovery that Dr. Hernandez had been in contact with Mr. Sanchez before the murder.

DR. HERNANDEZ BREAKS DOWN AND CONFESSES TO THE MURDER. HE REVEALS THAT HE HAD DISCOVERED MR. SANCHEZ'S ILLEGAL ACTIVITIES AND HAD CONFRONTED HIM ABOUT IT. WHEN MR. SANCHEZ THREATENED TO EXPOSE HIM, DR. HERNANDEZ LASHED OUT IN A FIT OF RAGE AND KILLED HIM.

AS THE TRAIN PULLS INTO ITS FINAL DESTINATION, ALEXANDER REFLECTS ON THE EVENTS OF THE PAST NIGHT. HE IS GRATEFUL FOR THE OPPORTUNITY TO HAVE SOLVED THE MYSTERY AND BROUGHT THE KILLER TO JUSTICE. AND AS HE STEPS OFF THE TRAIN, HE KNOWS THAT HE WILL NEVER FORGET THE GHOSTLY RIDE THROUGH THE MEXICAN MOUNTAINS AND THE MURDER THAT UNFOLDED ON THE TRACKS.

DR. ELENA RAMIREZ AND HER TEAM OF ARCHAEOLOGISTS: DR. RAMIREZ AND HER TEAM ARE EXPERTS IN MESOAMERICAN CIVILIZATIONS AND ARE ON THEIR WAY TO EXPLORE A NEWLY DISCOVERED ARCHAEOLOGICAL SITE IN THE REMOTE MOUNTAINS OF CENTRAL MEXICO. THEY HAVE A MOTIVE TO STOP MR. SANCHEZ FROM EXPLOITING ANCIENT ARTIFACTS, AS THEY BELIEVE THAT SUCH ACTIONS COULD DESTROY VALUABLE HISTORICAL INFORMATION AND DAMAGE THE INTEGRITY OF THE SITE.

THE MYSTERIOUS WOMAN IN BLACK: THE MYSTERIOUS WOMAN IN BLACK IS A ENIGMATIC FIGURE WHO SITS ALONE IN THE CORNER OF THE TRAIN CAR, HER EYES HIDDEN BEHIND DARK SUNGLASSES. SHE IS ELUSIVE AND KEEPS TO HERSELF, BUT ALEXANDER SENSES THAT SHE HAS A SECRET CONNECTION TO MR. SANCHEZ. COULD SHE BE THE KILLER, SEEKING REVENGE FOR A PAST WRONG?

THE WEALTHY BUSINESSMAN, MR. RODRIGO SANCHEZ: MR. SANCHEZ IS A WEALTHY BUSINESSMAN WHO IS TRAVELING WITH HIS ENTOURAGE OF BODYGUARDS AND ASSISTANTS. HE HAS A REPUTATION FOR BEING RUTHLESS AND AMBITIOUS, AND ALEXANDER DISCOVERS THAT HE HAD BEEN INVOLVED IN ILLEGAL ANTIQUITIES TRAFFICKING. COULD ONE OF HIS ENEMIES HAVE FOLLOWED HIM ONTO THE TRAIN AND KILLED HIM IN A FIT OF RAGE?

THE TRAIN CREW: THE TRAIN CREW ARE RESPONSIBLE FOR THE SAFETY AND OPERATION OF THE TRAIN. THEY HAVE ACCESS TO THE TRAIN'S COMPARTMENTS AND COULD HAVE HAD THE OPPORTUNITY TO COMMIT THE MURDER. HOWEVER, ALEXANDER FINDS NO EVIDENCE TO SUGGEST THAT ANY OF THE CREW MEMBERS HAD A MOTIVE TO HARM MR. SANCHEZ.

AS ALEXANDER CONTINUES HIS INVESTIGATION, HE CAREFULLY CONSIDERS EACH OF THE SUSPECTS AND THEIR POTENTIAL MOTIVES. HE KNOWS THAT THE KILLER COULD BE ANYONE, AND HE MUST ACT QUICKLY TO SOLVE THE CASE BEFORE THE TRAIN REACHES ITS FINAL DESTINATION.

As Alexander delves deeper into the investigation, he uncovers a shocking revelation: the murder was not committed by any of the passengers or the train crew. The real killer is a ghost from the past, seeking revenge for the desecration of ancient ruins.

Alexander discovers that the train is passing through an area that was once home to a powerful Mesoamerican civilization. The ancient ruins that dot the landscape are sacred to the spirits of the people who once inhabited them, and they are angered by the exploitation and destruction of their heritage.

THE GHOST OF A POWERFUL WARRIOR, WHO WAS ONCE A LEADER OF THE ANCIENT CIVILIZATION, HAS TAKEN IT UPON HIMSELF TO PROTECT THE RUINS AND PUNISH THOSE WHO SEEK TO EXPLOIT THEM. HE HAS BEEN HAUNTING THE TRAIN, SEEKING OUT THOSE WHO ARE RESPONSIBLE FOR THE DESTRUCTION OF HIS PEOPLE'S HERITAGE.

AS ALEXANDER CONFRONTS THE GHOST, HE REALIZES THAT HE MUST CONVINCE HIM TO MOVE ON PEACEFULLY. HE SHARES TALES OF HIS OWN RESPECT FOR HISTORY AND THE IMPORTANCE OF PRESERVING THE PAST FOR FUTURE GENERATIONS. HE PLEADS WITH THE GHOST TO LET GO OF HIS ANGER AND FIND PEACE.

FINALLY, THE GHOST RELENTS AND AGREES TO MOVE ON. THE TRAIN CONTINUES ITS
JOURNEY THROUGH MEXICO, NOW FREE FROM THE GHOST'S CURSE. ALEXANDER
REFLECTS ON THE EVENTS OF THE PAST NIGHT AND THE LESSONS LEARNED ABOUT
RESPECTING THE PAST AND THE CONSEQUENCES OF GREED.

AND AS HE STEPS OFF THE TRAIN, HE KNOWS THAT HE WILL NEVER FORGET THE
GHOSTLY RIDE THROUGH THE MEXICAN MOUNTAINS AND THE MURDER THAT UNFOLDED
ON THE TRACKS. BUT HE IS GRATEFUL FOR THE OPPORTUNITY TO HAVE SOLVED THE
MYSTERY AND BROUGHT PEACE TO THE RESTLESS SPIRIT.

AS ALEXANDER CONFRONTS THE GHOST, HE REALIZES THAT HE MUST CONVINCE HIM TO MOVE ON PEACEFULLY. HE SHARES TALES OF HIS OWN RESPECT FOR HISTORY AND THE IMPORTANCE OF PRESERVING THE PAST FOR FUTURE GENERATIONS. HE PLEADS WITH THE GHOST TO LET GO OF HIS ANGER AND FIND PEACE.

FINALLY, THE GHOST RELENTS AND AGREES TO MOVE ON. THE TRAIN CONTINUES ITS JOURNEY THROUGH MEXICO, NOW FREE FROM THE GHOST'S CURSE. ALEXANDER REFLECTS ON THE EVENTS OF THE PAST NIGHT AND THE LESSONS LEARNED ABOUT RESPECTING THE PAST AND THE CONSEQUENCES OF GREED.

AND AS HE STEPS OFF THE TRAIN, HE KNOWS THAT HE WILL NEVER FORGET THE GHOSTLY RIDE THROUGH THE MEXICAN MOUNTAINS AND THE MURDER THAT UNFOLDED ON THE TRACKS. BUT HE IS GRATEFUL FOR THE OPPORTUNITY TO HAVE SOLVED THE MYSTERY AND BROUGHT PEACE TO THE RESTLESS SPIRIT.

AS THE TRAIN PULLS INTO ITS FINAL DESTINATION, ALEXANDER REFLECTS ON THE EVENTS OF THE PAST NIGHT. HE IS GRATEFUL FOR THE OPPORTUNITY TO HAVE SOLVED THE MYSTERY AND BROUGHT THE RESTLESS SPIRIT TO PEACE. HE KNOWS THAT HE WILL NEVER FORGET THE GHOSTLY RIDE THROUGH THE MEXICAN MOUNTAINS AND THE MURDER THAT UNFOLDED ON THE TRACKS.

AS HE STEPS OFF THE TRAIN, ALEXANDER IS GREETED BY THE WARM HOSPITALITY OF THE LOCALS AND THE VIBRANT ENERGY OF THE CITY. HE IS GRATEFUL FOR THE CHANCE TO EXPLORE THE RICH HISTORY AND CULTURE OF MEXICO, AND HE KNOWS THAT HE WILL ALWAYS CARRY THE MEMORIES OF HIS ADVENTURE WITH HIM.

AS HE MAKES HIS WAY TO THE CONFERENCE TO GIVE HIS LECTURE, ALEXANDER IS FILLED WITH A SENSE OF ACCOMPLISHMENT AND PRIDE. HE KNOWS THAT HE HAS MADE A DIFFERENCE, AND HE IS EXCITED TO SHARE HIS EXPERIENCES WITH OTHERS.

AND AS HE STANDS BEFORE THE AUDIENCE, ALEXANDER BEGINS TO SPEAK. HE TELLS THEM OF THE GHOST TRAIN OF MEXICO AND THE MURDER THAT UNFOLDED ON ITS TRACKS. HE SHARES THE LESSONS HE LEARNED ABOUT RESPECTING THE PAST AND THE CONSEQUENCES OF GREED. AND HE REMINDS THEM THAT HISTORY IS NOT JUST A COLLECTION OF FACTS AND ARTIFACTS, BUT A LIVING, BREATHING STORY THAT WE ALL PLAY A PART IN.

AND AS ALEXANDER LEAVES THE CONFERENCE, HE KNOWS THAT HE WILL ALWAYS BE REMEMBERED AS THE MAN WHO SOLVED THE MYSTERY OF THE GHOST TRAIN OF MEXICO. AND HE KNOWS THAT HE WILL ALWAYS CARRY THE MEMORIES OF HIS ADVENTURE WITH HIM, A REMINDER OF THE POWER OF HISTORY AND THE IMPORTANCE OF PRESERVING THE PAST FOR FUTURE GENERATIONS.